Berkshire Contiguous Parishes

Copyright © C E Allen & R J Thompson 199?

Published by
CART Publications
66 Northern Road, Aylesbury, Bucks HP19 9QY

First edition 1997
Reprinted 1999 & 2000

ISBN 1 901824 00 4

This guide lists all parishes alphabetically with their adjoining parishes and hopefully will assist researchers to more readily organise their search patterns. Where Parishes are contiguous with other Counties these are shown using the Chapman County Codes.

ABINGDON St Helen	Sandford; Marcham; Besselsleigh; Wootton; Sunningwell; Abingdon St Nicholas; Sutton Courtenay; Drayton	
ABINGDON St Nicholas	Abingdon St Helen; Sunningwell; Radley; Sutton Courtenay; Culham (OXF); Nuneham Courtenay (OXF)	
ALDERMASTON	Wasing; Woolhampton; Bucklebury; Beenham; Padworth; Pamber (HAM); Tadley (HAM); Baughurst (HAM)	
ALDWORTH	Blewbury; Aston Tirrold; Cholsey; Moulsford; Streatley; Ashampstead; Hampstead Norris; Compton	
APPLEFORD	Sutton Courtney; Long Wittenham; Clifton Hampden (OXF); Culham (OXF)	
APPLETON	Cumnor; Besselleigh; Marcham; Fyfield; Stanton Harcourt (OXF); Northmoor (OXF)	
ARBORFIELD	Sonning; Hurst; Barkfield; Finchampstead; Swallowfield; Shinfield	
ARDINGTON	Wantage; West Hanney; East Hendred; West Hendred; East Lockinge; Farnborough	
ASHAMPSTEAD	Aldworth; Streatley; Basildon; Bradfield; Stanford Dingley; Yatterdon; Hampstead Norris	
ASHBURY	Shrivenham; Compton Beauchamp; Lambourn; Baydon (WIL); Bishopstone (WIL)	
ASTON TIRROLD	Blewbury; Aldworth; South Moreton; Aston Upthorp; Cholsey	
ASTON UPTHORP	South Moreton; Cholsey; Aston Tirrold	
AVINGTON	East Shefford; Kintbury; West Shefford; Hungerford	
BAGLEY WOOD	South HInksey; Kennington; Radley; Sunningwell	
BARKHAM	Hurst; Wokingham; Finchampstead; Arborfield	
BASILDON	Streatley; Ashampstead; Bradfield; Pangbourne; Goring (OXF); Whitchurch (OXF)	
BAULKING	Uffington; Shellingford	
BEEDON	East Ilsey; Hampstead Norris; Chieveley; Peasemore; Catmore	
BEENHAM	Bucklebury; Bradfield; Ufton Nervet; Padworth; Aldermaston; Woolhampton	
BESSELSLEIGH	Appleton; Cumnor; Wootton; Sandford; Abingdon St Helens; Marcham	
BINFIELD	Waltham St Lawrence; Shottesbrook; White Waltham; Warfield; Easthampstead; Wokingham	
BISHAM	Cookham; Maidenhead; White Waltham; Hurley; Great Marlow (BKM)	
BLEWBURY	Upton; Chilton; East Hagbourne; South Moreton; Aston Tirrold; Aldworth; Compton; East Ilsey	
BOXFORD	Welham; Leckhamstead; Peasemore; Winterbourne; Speen	
BRADFIELD	Ashamstead; Basildon; Pangbourne; Englefield; Ufton Nervet; Beenham; Bucklebury; Stanford Dingley	
BRAY	Maidenhead; Cookham; New Windsor; Clewer; Winkfield; Warfield; White Waltham; Taplow (BKM); Dorney (BKM); Burnham (BKM)	
BRIGHTWALTON	Wantage; Farnborough; Catmore; Peasemore; Leckhamstead; Chaddleworth; Fawley; Letcombe Regis	
BRIGHTWELL	Long Wittenham; Little Wittenham; North Moreton; South Moreton; Cholsey; Wallingford All Hallows; Wallingford St Mary; Wallingford St Leonard; Sotwell; Dorchester (OXF)	
BRIMPTON	Thatcham; Woolhampton; Wasing; Kingsclere (HAM)	
BUCKLAND	Great Farringdon; Hatford; Stanford in the Vale; Longworth; Pusey; Hinton Waldrist; Bampton (OXF)	
BUCKLEBURY	Hampstead Norris; Yatterdon; Frilsham; Stanford Dingley; Bradfield; Beenham; Aldermaston; Woolhampton; Thatcham; Midgham	
BURGHFIELD	Tilehurst; Reading St Mary; Reading St Giles; Shinfield; Sulhampstead Bannister; Sulhampstead Abbots; Stratfield Mortimer	
BUSCOT	Eaton Hastings; Great Coxwell; Coleshill; Kelmscott (OXF); Highworth (WIL); Inglesham (WIL)	

CATMORE	Farnborough; West Ilsey; East Ilsey; Beedon; Peasemore; Brightwalton
CHADDLEWORTH	Brightwalton; Leckhamstead; Welford; East Shefford; West Shefford; Fawley
CHARNEY BASSETT	Longworth; Stanworth in the Vale; Hinton Waldrist; Pusey
CHIEVELEY	Peasemore; Beedon; Hampstead Norris; Thatcham; Shaw cum Donnington; Winterbourne
CHILDREY	Goosey; Stanford in the Vale; Letcombe Regis; West Challow; Letcombe Bassett; Lambourn; Sparsholt
CHILTON	East Hendred; Harwell; East Hagbourne; Upton; Blewbury; East Ilsey; West Ilsey
CHOLSEY	Brightwell; Sotwell; Wallingford St Leonard; Moulsford; Aldworth; Aston Tirrold; Aston Upthorp; South Moreton; Mongewell (OXF); North Stoke (OXF); Ipsden (OXF); Checkenden (OXF); South Stoke (OXF)
CLEWER	New Windsor; Bray; Winkfield; Eton (BKM)
COLESHILL	Buscot; Great Coxwell; Watchfield; Shrivenham; Highworth (WIL); Sevenhampton (WIL)
COMPTON	Blewbury; Aldworth; Hampstead Norris; East Ilsey
COMPTON BEAUCHAMP	Shrivenham; Uffington; Woolstone; Lambourne; Ashbury
COOKHAM	Maidenhead; Bray; White Waltham; Bisham; Great Marlow (BKM); Little Marlow (BKM); Wooburn (BKM); Hedsor (BKM); Taplow (BKM)
CUMNOR	Wytham; North Hinksey; South Hinksey; Sunningwell; Wootton; Appleton; Besselsleigh; Cassington (OXF); Eynsham (OXF); Stanton Harcourt (OXF)
DENCHWORTH	West Hanney; Letcombe Regis; Goosey; Stanford in the Vale; Charney Bassett; Longworth
DIDCOT	Sutton Courtenay; Long Wittenham; South Moreton; East Hagbourne; Harwell
DRAYTON	Sutton Courtney; Marcham; Milton; Steventon; Abingdon St Helen; West Hanney
EAST CHALLOW	Wantage; West Challow; Letcombe Regis
EAST GARSTON	Lambourn; Letcombe Bassett; Fawley; West Shefford; Hungerford; Chilton Foliat (WIL)
EAST HAGBOURNE	Harwell; Didcot; South Moreton; Blewbury; Upton; Chilton
EAST HAMPSTEAD	Wokingham; Binfield; Warfield; Winkfield; Sandhurst; Frimley (SRY); Ash (SRY)
EAST HENDRED	West Hanney; Wantage; Ardington; West Hendred; Steventon; Milton; Harwell; Chilton; West Ilsey
EAST ILSEY	West Ilsey; Chilton; Blewbury; Compton; Hampstead Norris; Beedon; Catmore
EAST LOCKINGE	Wantage; West Hanney; Ardington; West Hendred; West Ilsey; Farnborough
EAST SHEFFORD	West Shefford; Chaddleworth; Welford; Kintbury; Avington
EATON HASTINGS	Buscot; Great Coxwell; Great Faringdon; Kelmscott (OXF); Langford (OXF)
ENBORNE	Hamstead Marshall; Speen; Newbury; Highclere (HAM); East Woodhay (HAM)
ENGLEFIELD	Bradfield; Pangbourne; Sulham; Tilehurst; Sulhampstead Bannister; Sulhampstead Abbots; Ufton Nervet

FARNBOROUGH	Wantage; East Lockinge; Ardington; West Ilsey; Catmore; Brightwalton
FAWLEY	Letcombe Regis; Wantage; Brightwalton; Chaddleworth; West Shefford; East Garston; Letcombe Bassett
FINCHAMPSTEAD	Swallowfield; Arborfield; Barkham; Wokingham; Sandhurst; Eversley (HAM)
FRILFORD	Marcham
FRILSHAM	Yatterdon; Stanford Dingley; Bucklebury; Hampstead Norris
FYFIELD	Appleton; Marcham; Garford; West Hanney; Kingston Bagpuze
GARFORD	Marcham; Fyfield
GOOSEY	Stanford in the Vale; Denchworth; Letcombe Regis
GREAT COXWELL	Eaton Hastings; Little Coxwell; Great Faringdon; Shrivenham; Coleshill; Buscot
GREAT FARINGDON	Buckland; Hatford; Stanford in the Vale; Shellingford; Shrivenham; Little Coxwell; Great Coxwell; Eaton Hatings; Longford (OXF); Clanfield (OXF); Bampton (OXF)
GREENHAM	Thatcham; Newbury; Sandleford
HAMPSTEAD MARSHALL	West Woodhay; Kintbury; Welford; Speen; Enborne; East Woodhay (HAM)
HAMPSTEAD NORRIS	East Ilsey; Compton; Aldworth; Ashampstead; Yattendon; Frilsham; Bucklebury; Thatcham; Chievely; Beedon
HARWELL	Milton; Sutton Courtenay; Didcot; East Hagbourne; Chilton; East Hendred
HATFORD	Great Faringdon; Buckland; Stanford in the Vale
HINTON WALDRIST	Longworth; Charney Bassett; Pusey; Buckland; Shifford (OXF); Bampton (OXF)
HUNGERFORD	East Garston; West Shefford; Avington; Kintbury; Inkpen; Shalbourne; Chilton Foliat (WIL); Ramsbury (WIL); Froxfield (WIL)
HURLEY	Bisham; White Waltham; Shottesbrook; Waltham St Lawrence; Wargrave; Great Marlow (BKM)
HURST	Sonning; Wargrave; Ruscombe; Waltham St Lawrence; Wokingham; Barkham; Arborfield; Shinfield
INKPEN	Hungerford; Kintbury; West Woodhay; Shalbourne; Ham (WIL); Buttermere (WIL); Vernham Dean (HAM)
KENNINGTON	Radley; Bagley Wood; Sandford on Thames (OXF); Littlemore (OXF)
KINGSTON BAGPUZE	Fyfield; Marcham; West Hanney; Longworth; North Moor (OXF)
KINGSTON LISLE	Sparsholt
KINTBURY	West Shefford; Avington; East Shefford; Welford; Wickham; Hampstead Marshall; West Woodhay; Inkpen; Hungerford
LAMBOURN	Ashbury; Compton Beauchamp; Uffington; Sparsholt; Childrey; Letcombe Bassett; East Garston; Chilton Foliat (WIL); Bayden (WIL); Ramsbury (WIL)
LECKHAMSTEAD	Chaddleworth; Brightwalton; Peasmore; Winterbourne; Boxford; Welford
LETCOMBE BASSETT	Childrey; Letcombe Regis; Fawley; East Garston; Lambourn
LETCOMBE REGIS	Goosey; Stanford in the Vale; Denchworth; West Hanney; Wantage; East Challow; West Challow; Brightwalton; Fawley; Letcombe Bassett; Childrey
LITTLE COXWELL	Great Faringdon; Great Coxwell
LITTLE WITTENHAM	Long Wittenham; North Moreton; Brightwell; Dorchester (OXF)

LONGCOT	Shrivenham; Uffington
LONG WITTENHAM	Appleford; Sutton Courtenay; Didcot; South Moreton; North Moreton; Brightwell; Little Wittenham; Clifton Hampden (OXF); Dorchester (OXF)
LONGWORTH	Kingston Bagpuze; Lyford; West Hanney; Charney Bassett; Denchworth; Stanford in the Vale; Buckland; Pusey; Hinton Waldrist; Shifford (OXF); Bampton (OXF)
LYFORD	West Hanney; Longworth
MAIDENHEAD	Cookham; Bray
MARCHAM	Frilford; Garford; Appleton; Besselsleigh; Abingdon St Helens; Sutton Courtenay; Drayton; West Hanney; Kingston Bagpuze; Fyfield
MIDGHAM	Thatcham; Bucklebury
MILTON	Drayton; Sutton Courtney; Harwell; East Hendred; Steventon
MOULSFORD	Cholsey; Aldworth; Streatley; South Stoke (OXF)
NEWBURY	Enborne; Speen; Thatcham; Greenham; Sandleford; Newtown (HAM); Burghclere (HAM)
NEW WINDSOR	Bray; Clewer; Old Windsor; Winkfield; Datchet (BKM); Eton (BKM); Upton (BKM); Burnham (BKM)
NORTH HINKSEY	Wytham; Cumnor; South Hinksey; Binsey (OXF); Oxford (OXF)
NORTH MORETON	Long Wittenham; Little Wittenham; Brightwell; South Moreton
OLD WINDSOR	New Windsor; Winkfield; Sunninghill; Wraysbury (BKM); Datchet (BKM); Windlesham (SRY); Egham (SRY)
PADWORTH	Aldermaston; Beenham; Ufton Nervet; Stratfield Mortimer; Silchester (HAM); Pamber (HAM)
PANGBOURNE	Basildon; Bradfield; Englefield; Tidmarsh; Sulham; Purley; Whitchurch (OXF)
PEASEMORE	Catmore; Beedon; Chieveley; Winterbourne; Boxford; Leckhamstead; Brightwalton
PURLEY	Pangbourne; Tidmarsh; Sulham; Tilehurst; Whitchurch (OXF); Mapledurham (OXF)
PUSEY	Buckland; Hinton Waldrist; Longworth; Charney Bassett
RADLEY	Kennington; South Hinksey; Bagley Wood; Abingdon St Nicholas; Sunningwell; Culham (OXF); Nuneham Courtenay (OXF); Sandford on Thames (OXF); Littlemore (OXF); Iffley (OXF)
READING St Giles	Reading St Mary; Reading St Lawrence; Sonning; Shinfield; Burghfield
READING St Lawrence	Reading St Mary; Sonning; Reading St Giles; Caversham (OXF)
READING St Mary	Reading St Lawrence; Reading St Giles; Burghfield; Tilehurst; Caversham (OXF); Mapledurham (OXF)
REMENHAM	Wargrave; Fawley (BKM); Hambleden (BKM); Henley (OXF); Rotherfield Greys (OXF); Rotherfield Peppard (OXF); Harpsden (OXF)
RUSCOMBE	Wargrave; Waltham St Lawrence; Hurst

SANDFORD	Besselsleigh; Abingdon St Helen
SANDHURST	Finchampstead; Wokingham; Easthampstead; Yateley (HAM); Ash (SRY); Winkfield
SANDLEFORD	Newbury; Greenham; Thatcham; Newtown (HAM); Burghclere (HAM)
SHAW CUM DONNINGTON	Winterbourne; Chieveley; Thatcham; Speen
SHELLINGFORD	Great Faringdon; Stanford in the Vale; Baulking; Uffington; Shrivenham
SHINFIELD	Burghfield; Reading St Giles; Sonning; Hurst; Arborfield; Swallowfield; Sulhampstead Abbots; Stratfield Mortimer; Stratfield Saye (HAM)
SHOTTESBROOK	Hurley; White Waltham; Binfield; Waltham St Lawrence
SHRIVENHAM	Watchfield; Longcot; Coleshill; Great Coxwell; Great Faringdon; Shellingford; Uffington; Compton Beauchamp; Ashbury; Bishopstone (WIL); Little Hinton (WIL); Highworth (WIL); South Marston (WIL); Sevenhampton (WIL)
SONNING	Reading St Lawrence; Reading St Giles; Shinfield; Arborfield; Hurst; Wargrave; Caversham (OXF); Checkendon (OXF); Shiplake (OXF); Rotherfield Peppard (OXF)
SOTWELL	Brightwell; Wallingford All Hallows; Cholsey; Dorchester (OXF); Warborough (OXF)
SOUTH HINKSEY	North Hinksey; Cumnor; Bagley Wood; Kennington; Radley; Sunningwell; Iffley (OXF); Oxford (OXF)
SOUTH MORETON	Long Wittenham; North Moreton; Brightwell; Cholsey; Aston Upthorp; Aston Tirrold; Blewbury; East Hagbourne; Didcot
SPARSHOLT	Kinston Lisle; Uffington; Stanford in the Vale; Childrey; Lambourn
SPEEN	Welford; Boxford; Winterbourne; Shaw cum Donnington; Thatcham; Newbury; Enborne; Hampstead Marshall
STANFORD DINGLEY	Frilsham; Yattendon; Ashampstead; Bradfield; Bucklebury
STANFORD IN THE VALE	Goosey; Great Faringdon; Hatford; Buckland; Longworth; Charney Bassett; Benchworth; Letcombe Regis; Childrey; Sparsholt; Uffington; Shellingford
STEVENTON	West Hanney; Sutton Courtney; Drayton; Milton; East Hendred; West Hendred
STRATFIELD MORTIMER	Ufton Nervet; Sulhampstead Abbots; Sulhampstead Bannister; Burghfield; Shinfield; Stratfield Saye (HAM); Silcheater (HAM); Pamber (HAM)
STREATLEY	Aldworth; Moulsford; Ashampstead; Basildon; South Stoke (OXF); Goring (OXF)
SULHAM	Pangbourne; Purley; Tilehurst; Tidmarsh
SULHAMPSTEAD ABBOTS	Englefield; Ufton Nervet; Stratfield Mortimer; Sulhampstead Bannister; Tilehurst;Burghfield; Shinfield; Stratfield Saye (HAM)
SULHAMPSTEAD BANNISTER	Sulhampstead Abbots; Stratfield Mortimer; Ufton Nervet; Englefield
SUNNINGHILL	Old Windsor; Winkfield
SUNNINGWELL	Wootton; Cumnor; South Hinksey; Bagley Wood; Radley; Abingdon St Nicholas; Abingdon St Helen
SUTTON COURTENAY	West Hanney; Drayton; Steventon; Marcham; Abingdon St Helen; Milton; Abingdon St Nicholas; Harwell; Appleford; Didcot; Long Wittenham; Clifton Hampden (OXF); Culham (OXF)
SWALLOWFIELD	Shinfield; Arborfield; Finchampstead; Stratfield Saye (HAM); Heckfield (HAM); Eversley (HAM)
THATCHAM	Greenham; Midgham; Sandleford; Newbury; Speen; Shaw cum Donnington; Chieveley; Hampstead Norris; Bucklebury; Woolhampton; Brimpton; Kingsclere (HAM)
TIDMARSH	Pangbourne; Sulham; Tilehurst; Englefield
TILEHURST	Purley; Reading St Mary; Burghfield; Sulhampstead Abbots; Englefield; Tidmarsh; Sulham; Mapledurham (OXF); Caversham (OXF)

UFFINGTON	Baulking; Wolstone; Longcot; Shrivenham; Shellingford; Stanford in the Vale; Sparsholt; Lambourn; Compton Beauchamp
UFTON NERVET	Bradfield; Englefield; Sulhampstead Bannister; Sulhampstead Abbots; Stratfield Mortimer; Padworth; Beenham; Silchester (HAM); Pamber (HAM)
UPTON	Blewbury; East Hagbourne; Chilton
WALLINGFORD All Hallows	Sotwell; Brightwell; Wallington St Peter; Wallingford St Mary; Warborough (OXF); Benson (OXF); Crowmarsh Gifford (OXF)
WALLINGFORD St Leonard	Brightwell; Wallingford St Mary; Wallingford St Peter; Cholsey; Mongwell (OXF)
WALLINGFORD St Mary	Wallingford All Hallows; Wallingford St Peter; Wallingford St Leonard; Brightwell
WALLINGFORD St Peter	Wallingford All Hallows; Wallingford St Mary; Wallingford St Leonard; Newnham Murren (OXF)
WALTHAM ST LAWRENCE	Wargrave; Hurley; Shottesbrook; Binfield; Wokingham; Hurst; Ruscombe
WANTAGE	West Hanney; East Lockinge; Ardington; East Hendred; East Challow; West Hendred; Farnborough; Broghtwalton; Fawley; Letcombe Regis
WARFIELD	White Waltham; Bray; Winkfield; Easthampstead; Binfield
WARGRAVE	Remenham; Hambleden (BKM); Medmenham (BKM); Hurley; Waltham St Lawrence; Ruscombe; Hurst; Sonning; Shiplake (OXF); Rotherfield Greys (OXF); Henley (OXF)
WASING	Brimpton; Woolhampton; Aldermaston; Baughurst (HAM)
WATCHFIELD	Shrivenham; Coleshill
WELFORD	Wickham; East Shefford; Chaddleworth; Leckhamstead; Boxford; Speen; Hampstead Marshall; Kintbury
WEST CHALLOW	Letcombe Regis; East Challow; Childrey
WEST HENDRED	Wantage; East Hendred; Steventon; West Ilsey; East Lockinge; Ardington
WEST HANNEY	Lyford; Letcombe Regis; Denchworth; Longworth; Kingston Bagpuze; Fyfield; Marcham; Drayton; Sutton Courtney; Steventon; East Hendred; Ardington; East Lockinge; Wantage
WEST ILSEY	West Hendred; East Hendred; Chilton; East Ilsey; Catmore; Farnborough; East Lockinge
WEST SHEFFORD	East Garston; Fawley; Chaddleworth; East Shefford; Avington; Kintbury; Hungerford
WEST WOODHAY	Inkpen; Kintbury; Hampstead Marshall; Coombe (HAM); East Woodhay (HAM)
WHITE WALTHAM	Bisham; Cookham; Bray; Warfield; Binfield; Shottesbrook; Hurley
WICKHAM	Welford; Kintbury
WINKFIELD	Bray; Warfield; Clewer; New Windsor; Old Windsor; Easthampstead; Sunninghill; Sandhurst; Ash (SRY); Windlesham (SRY)
WINTERBOURNE	Leckhamstead; Peasemore; Chieveley; Shaw cum Donnington; Speen; Boxford
WOKINGHAM	Hurst; Waltham St Lawrence; Binfield; Easthampstead; Sandhurst; Finchampstead; Barkham
WOLSTONE	Uffington; Compton Beauchamp
WOOLHAMPTON	Bucklebury; Aldermaston; Beenham; Wasing; Brimpton; Thatcham
WOOTTON	Cumnor; Sunningwell; Abingdon St Helen; Besselsleigh
WYTHAM	Cumnor; North Hinksey; Yarnton (OXF); Wolvercote (OXF); Binsey (OXF); Oxford (OXF); Cassington (OXF)
YATTENDON	Hampstead Norris; Ashampstead; Stanford Dingley; Frilsham; Bucklebury